The
Perfected
Heart

The Perfected Heart

by
Billy Rash

HARRISON HOUSE
Tulsa, Oklahoma

Unless otherwise indicated,
all Scripture quotations are taken from
the *King James Version* of the Bible.

2nd Printing
Over 10,000 in Print

The Perfected Heart
ISBN 0-89274-300-X
Copyright © 1983 by Billy Rash
P. O. Box 79506
Fort Worth, Texas 76179

Published by Harrison House, Inc.
P. O. Box 35035
Tulsa, Oklahoma 74153

Contents

1 God Is Seeking A Perfect Heart   7

2 Old Testament Examples   13

3 Being Perfect Toward God   25

4 Being Perfect As God   37

5 A Heart Like God's   45

6 Perfect In Christ Jesus   67

7 Perfection As A Seed   77

8 The Perfect Tongue   87

Conclusion   93

1
God Is Seeking
A Perfect Heart

For the eyes of the Lord run to and fro throughout the whole earth, to shew himself strong in behalf of them whose heart is perfect toward him.

2 Chronicles 16:9

Every minute of every day, God is searching the earth. His eyes are continually looking for people to whom He can show Himself strong. One translation says, ''The eyes of the Lord are darting to and fro throughout the whole earth looking . . . .''

One thing will cause God to show Himself strong in the lives of believers:

a perfect heart. God looks on a person's heart, not on his works.

All of us have missed the mark at some time in our lives. Yet, God seems to bless us in spite of our mistakes and failures.

As I was studying the principle of God's blessing upon His people, I read about Israel's King Saul. When Saul's anointing was removed from him, God sent the prophet Samuel to the house of Jesse to anoint one of Jesse's sons as the next king of Israel. Instead of telling Samuel which son was to be king, God had him call each one forward, beginning with the eldest. As each boy was called, God would say, "No, that's not the one." Finally, there was only one son left—David, the shepherd boy.

By studying this story, I began to understand how God operates. He said to Samuel, "I don't look on the outward man; I look on the heart." (1 Sam. 16:7.)

God is looking for a person who will keep a perfect heart before Him.

God's Definition of The Perfect Heart

The word *perfect* is used over 130 times in the Bible—79 times in the Old Testament, 51 times in the New Testament. The use of the word *perfect* by the writers of both testaments was not at all absolute or definitive.

In Old Testament Hebrew, *perfect* many times means full or complete. In New Testament Greek, it means mature, or without spot or blemish. Neither of these fully defines the concept of perfection as God views it.

Realizing this, I prayed to God for a definition that would combine both Hebrew and Greek in such a way as to fully describe how God wants His people to be. The Lord gave me this: A heart that is perfect toward God is a

9

heart from which all that is wrong has been removed, and to which all that is wanting has been supplied.

How To Please God

In our opening scripture, 2 Chronicles 16:9, there are three points we need to see:

1. God is looking to show Himself strong.

Contrary to some teachings, God is not sitting in heaven with a big stick, looking for someone He can bash in the head. He wants to bless His people and show Himself strong in their behalf.

2. We must rely on and trust in God.

The New Testament puts it this way:

But without faith it is impossible to please him: for he that cometh to God must believe that he is, and that he is a rewarder of them that diligently seek him.

Hebrews 11:6

3. We must have a perfect heart.

God wants us to perfect our works. He wants us to get our lives in line with His Word—to do the Word, to put action to our faith. When you fail in any area, remember this: God is looking on the intent of your heart, not on your failure. Always keep your heart upright and sincere before Him. When you miss it, be quick to repent.

Get these three elements operating in your behalf and God will move in ways you can't even imagine. Remember though, this isn't something you do occasionally; it's a way of life that you must walk in every day.

2

Old Testament Examples

Many people in the Old Testament had a perfect heart toward God. Let's look at some of them.

Abraham

And when Abram was ninety years old and nine, the Lord appeared to Abram, and said unto him, I am the Almighty God . . . .
Genesis 17:1

God identifies Himself to Abraham as *El Shaddai*. In Hebrew, that means the Breasty One, the Supreme Provider Who supplies all our needs.

He goes on to say: *Walk before me, and be thou perfect* (v. 1). This literally means,

13

"Walk before Me, and be upright and sincere." There is more required of Abraham than just to recognize God as *El Shaddai*. He must walk before Him and be perfect.

Remember the three aspects of 2 Chronicles 16:9. We see them here in Genesis 17:1. God was saying to Abraham, "I am the Supreme Provider of all your needs. Everything is supplied in Me. I will show Myself strong in your behalf." He says, "Walk before Me, trust in Me, and be perfect."

Then the Lord says, *And I will make my covenant between me and thee* (v. 2). Abraham must have walked perfectly before God, because the covenant was made.

Abraham fellowshipped with God. He was called the friend of God. (James 2:23.) He walked before God, trusted in Him, and communed with Him.

14

But read about Abraham's life and you will see how many times he missed it. Yet, in spite of Abraham's failures, God looked at his heart and made a covenant of blessing with him.

To be blessed, as Abraham was, requires an intimate communion with God, a mutual sharing with Him of experiences, activities, and interests. Have that kind of fellowship and communion with God, with a perfect heart, and He will show Himself strong in your behalf.

Consider Not Your Body

As I studied God's promise to Abraham, I discovered that it took almost 25 years for Abraham's promised heir to appear. In Genesis 15:3-6 we read:

And Abram said, Behold, to me thou hast given no seed: and, lo, one born in my house is mine heir.

And, behold, the word of the Lord came unto him, saying, This shall not be thine heir; but he that shall come forth out of thine own bowels shall be thine heir.

And he brought him forth abroad, and said, Look now toward heaven, and tell the stars, if thou be able to number them: and he said unto him, So shall thy seed be.

And he believed in the Lord; and he counted it to him for righteousness.

Twenty-five years before the birth of Isaac, God told Abraham that his children would be as the stars of the heavens. That may have been hard for Abraham to believe. He was already an old man—74 or 75 years old at the time—with no children of his own, and no prospect of having any. His wife Sarah was not able to bear children.

After eleven years, Sarah, still unable to bear children of her own, gave her handmaiden Hagar to Abraham to bear him a child. Ishmael was born of that union. (Gen. 16:16.) That means Abraham's body was still alive and able to produce an offspring at age 86.

In Genesis, chapter 17, Abraham was 99 years old, so 13 more years had gone by. By that time he was unable to father children himself. But Romans 4:19 says that Abraham *considered not his own body now dead.*

It was physically impossible for Abraham and Sarah to produce a child. Yet, Abraham trusted and relied upon God with a perfect heart. He stood firm in faith regardless of the physical circumstances that were against him. He walked before God in fellowship, kept a perfect heart, and God showed Himself strong in his behalf.

God quickened (made alive) Abraham's body. He took the image, or vision, Abraham had in his heart concerning a son and changed it into a reality. Isaac came into being just as God had promised.

To walk before God with a perfect heart will produce miracles, no matter what the physical circumstances may be.

Hezekiah

In those days was Hezekiah sick unto death. And the prophet Isaiah the son of Amoz came to him, and said unto him, Thus saith the Lord, Set thine house in order; for thou shalt die, and not live.

Then he turned his face to the wall, and prayed unto the Lord, saying, I beseech thee, O Lord, remember now how I have walked before thee in truth and **with a perfect heart***, and have done that which is good in thy sight. And Hezekiah wept sore.*

And it came to pass, afore Isaiah was gone out into the middle court, that the word of the Lord came to him, saying, Turn again, and tell Hezekiah the captain of my people, Thus saith the Lord, the God of David thy father, I have heard thy prayer, I have seen thy tears: behold, I will heal thee:

on the third day thou shalt go up unto the house of the Lord.

And I will add unto thy days fifteen years; and I will deliver thee and this city out of the hand of Assyria; and I will defend this city for mine own sake, and for my servant David's sake.

2 Kings 20:1-6

Hezekiah was sick unto death, so Isaiah the prophet came to him. In those days, the voice of the prophet of God was the voice of God Himself. When the prophet spoke, people listened!

Now picture this. Isaiah walks in and delivers his message to Hezekiah. But before Isaiah can get out the back door, Hezekiah turns his face to the wall and prays: "Lord, I've walked upright before You with a perfect heart all the days of my life and have done that which was good in Your sight."

When God heard Hezekiah's prayer, He stopped Isaiah. He told him to go back to Hezekiah and say these words: *Thus saith the Lord . . . I have heard thy prayer, I have seen thy tears: behold, I will heal thee . . . And I will add unto thy days fifteen years.*

Hezekiah had become king at age 25 and had been reigning for 29 years when he became sick to death. That made him about 55 years old. (2 Kings 18:2.) According to Psalm 90:10, the child of God is promised three score and ten years (or seventy years), and if by reason of strength, eighty years. Hezekiah had a promised life span of at least 70 years, so he was too young to die. He took his promise and stood before God with it. On the basis of having walked uprightly before God with a perfect heart all the days of his life, Hezekiah was given his promised 70 years. Then he slept with his fathers. (2 Kings 20:21.)

I want us to notice some things about Hezekiah.

First, his prayer: *O Lord, remember . . .* (He immediately put God in remembrance.) *. . . now how I have walked before thee in truth and with a perfect heart, and have done that which is good in thy sight.*

Even though the prophet of the Lord had told Hezekiah he was going to die, he knew God was able to change the situation. So he appealed to Him.

The writer of Hebrews said almost the same thing: *For God is not unrighteous to forget your work and labour of love* (Heb. 6:10). God will not forget you and your work. Put Him in remembrance as Hezekiah did.

Secondly, Hezekiah reminded God of how he had walked before Him in fellowship. Thirdly, he reminded God that he had a perfect heart.

There was no hesitation on his part. There was a boldness in the prayer Hezekiah made. Even though he had missed it, he still had the boldness to stand before God and say, "I've walked before You with a perfect heart."

Let me show you why Hezekiah could stand so boldly before God.

He (Hezekiah) **did that which was right in the sight of the Lord,** *according to all that David his father did . . . .*

He **trusted in the Lord** *God of Israel; so that after him was none like him among all the kings of Judah, nor any that were before him.*

For he **clave to the Lord,** *and departed not from following him, but* **kept his commandments,** *which the Lord commanded Moses.*

And the Lord was with him; and he prospered whithersoever he went forth: and he rebelled against the king of Assyria, and served him not.

He smote the Philistines.

2 Kings 18:3,5-8

Hezekiah had fellowship and communion with God. He ministered to the Lord. He followed the Lord and kept His commandments. Because of that, God showed Himself strong in Hezekiah's behalf.

Noah

Genesis 6:9 says, *Noah was a just man and perfect in his generations.* Noah was literally a type and shadow of the Savior when he rode over the waves in the ark and brought forth the people. He had a perfect heart toward God. But then he left the ark, raised a vineyard, and got falling down drunk! (Gen. 9:21.) Noah's works were not yet perfect, but in God's eyes he had a perfect heart. For that reason, God could use him to deliver mankind from destruction.

David

As the king of Israel, David did some things that were less than perfect. He sent out one of his own soldiers and had him killed so that he could take his wife. But in spite of the things David did, God looked on his heart.

Years later, God told David's son, Solomon: ''You are not as your father, David, who walked before Me with a perfect heart.'' (1 Kings 11:4; 15:3.) He accounted David as having a perfect heart, even though some of his works were not at all perfect.

3

Being Perfect Toward God

There are some specific characteristics of a heart that is perfect toward God. Let's look at them.

1. Reliance upon God

Simply stated, a heart that is perfect toward God trusts Him.

In 2 Chronicles 16:8, when Asa, the king of Judah, relied on the Lord, his enemies were delivered into his hands. Because he trusted in God, God gave him the victory.

Romans 4:21 tells how Abraham was *fully persuaded* in his heart that God would give him a son as He had promised.

So it is with you and me. To have a perfected heart, we must be fully persuaded and trust in God completely, without reservation.

2. A Limitless Attitude Toward God

It's a mistake to limit God. In fact, it dishonors God for us to let the mere limitation of our ideals be the measure of our spiritual expectations. Ephesians 3:20 describes our God as One Who will do *exceeding abundantly above all that we ask or think.* No matter how big we can think, God can do more.

Don't limit Him by the measure of your thinking in the human realm. Think in line with God's Word. See yourself as God sees you. Believe in the right-standing you have before Him.

26

Stand on it by the faith you have in Jesus' name.

Don't allow Satan to accuse you and bring you under condemnation because of your failures. Some people hesitate to pray for others because of the mistakes they themselves have made.

Don't limit God by *your* expectations. Believe that He will perfect that which concerns you, even if you haven't always walked in perfection.

3. Boldness

The Apostle John had caught hold of an attitude of boldness when he wrote:

Beloved, if our heart condemn us not, then have we confidence toward God.

And whatsoever we ask, we receive of him, because we keep his commandments, and do those things that are pleasing in his sight.

1 John 3:21,22

Walk with a perfect heart toward God. Then, even though your works may not be perfected, your heart will not condemn you and you will have confidence toward God.

Do that which is pleasing in His sight. Even when you do sometimes fail, you can know that what you ask of Him you will receive.

The key to confidence and boldness before God is to keep your heart perfected. If you have certain traits working against you—little foxes that spoil the vines, areas where you miss it here and there—keep your heart right before God, remembering that He looks on your heart, not on your failures.

Many people in the Bible made stupid mistakes, yet God still called them perfect. If He did that for them, He will do it for you. Don't let your mistakes rob you of your boldness before God. God is still looking to show Himself strong in your behalf.

Be bold in prayer and in faith, and God will be bold in your behalf.

Abraham was bold. He called himself the friend of God. God gave him a new name and he was bold about using it. Never limit God by your thoughts, feelings, words, or your own self-image. Be bold before Him, and He will honor that boldness.

4. Avoidance of Iniquity

Psalm 18:23-32 says that a heart perfect toward God keeps itself from iniquity. The word *iniquity* literally means to use the forces of God in reverse. For instance, fear is the reverse or the opposite of faith. First John 4:18 says, *perfect love casteth out fear.* Fear is faith in reverse—faith in Satan and his power rather than in God and His ability.

Job 15:5 says, *Thy mouth uttereth thine iniquity.* It's with your mouth that iniquity comes in. So keep yourself from iniquity by watching your words, by keeping your heart cleansed of all unrighteousness.

5. Obedience

Hezekiah and Abraham kept God's commandments. They did that which was right in God's sight. You can't have a perfected heart if you practice disobedience to God's commandments.

To most people, obedience means doing what they are told. But scripturally there is more to it than that.

The word *obey* actually has three meanings: to hear, to comprehend, to execute. These are the three steps to Bible obedience. First, you must hear the command. Second, you must understand the command. Once you have heard and understood it, then you must execute it.

You can think you are in obedience, but have only two of these in operation.

Many people hear and understand, but don't do anything. Others hear and do, but don't understand why they are doing it.

There are four classes of people in the earth:

1. Those who hear the Word and do it.

2. Those who hear the Word, but don't do it.

3. Those who don't hear the Word, but try to do it anyway.

4. Those who neither hear the Word nor do it.

Each of us falls into one of these categories, regardless of how we may feel about it.

True obedience is to hear the command, to spend the time necessary to understand that command, and then once having heard and understood, to execute it.

Kenneth Hagin gives an excellent illustration of obedience. He tells the story of a farmer who was sitting under a big tree on his farm, looking up into the heavens, talking to God. Suddenly the letters **GP** appeared in the sky. Instantly he recognized that as a sign from God: **Go Preach.** So he sold his farm and went off to Africa to preach the Gospel.

He tried to preach there for a couple of years, but failed at everything he did. Finally he got so discouraged that he gave up and came home. Then he repented and said to God, "I don't understand. You said to go preach. I heard the command and obeyed it. What went wrong?"

The Lord spoke and said, "Son, you heard My command, but you didn't understand it. I wasn't telling you to go preach, I was telling you to go plow!"

The moral of this story is very simple. It isn't enough just to hear the command, you have to spend the time to understand it. Then when you understand what you have heard, you must execute it properly.

These three steps to obedience involve spirit, soul, and body. You can hear with your ears in the physical realm, with your mind in the soulish realm, and with your spirit in the spiritual realm.

6. Increase in the Knowledge of God's Will

All scripture is given by inspiration of God, and is profitable for doctrine, for reproof, for correction, for instruction in righteousness:

That the man of God may be perfect, throughly furnished unto all good works.
2 Timothy 3:16,17

God wants good works, but the perfecting comes first. He wants you perfect, and you can be perfect. The Word has been given to perfect you.

You may be intent on serving God with a perfect heart, but it is only to the measure of your knowledge of God's will that will enable you to operate in that perfection.

The more knowledge you have of God's will, the more perfected you will become. If you are truly seeking to know and do God's will, then you are being perfected, just as Jesus Himself was perfected in life.

Though he were a Son, yet learned he obedience by the things which he suffered;

And being made perfect, he became the author of eternal salvation unto all them that obey him.

Hebrews 5:8,9

Suppose a man is doing yard work. Because of his expert knowledge and experience, everything is being done just right. Then his eight-year-old son comes out of the house. He sees his father working, so he decides to get involved. He grabs a tool and starts to work. The work he does is far from perfect, but he tries hard and does the best he can.

The little boy had good intentions; his heart was in the right place. He wanted to help his father, even though the work he could do was not yet perfect.

It gave his father a thrill to see his son trying so hard to help. Though the boy's work was not perfect, the father overlooked the imperfection. He saw only the attitude of his son's heart. That is what God does with us as His children.

God's work is perfect; ours isn't. But that doesn't matter. If we will keep our hearts intent upon working with God and keep a perfect heart toward Him, He will overlook our works that are not yet fully developed. He will look only at our hearts.

When you start serving God, reaching out and doing things for Him, your work may not be perfect at first; you are still a child, still developing and learning.

As you are developing in Him and allowing Him to develop in you, you will do some things wrong, but keep your heart right. God will look at that and will show Himself strong in your behalf.

As your knowledge of God's will increases, your works will become more and more perfect. Eventually, you will find yourself able to serve God, not only with your heart, but also with your body and mind.

4

Being Perfect As God

Would you like to have a heart perfect **as** God? Well, you can!

In the fifth chapter of Matthew's Gospel, Jesus delivers a message to His disciples known as "The Sermon on the Mount." This is not really a beatitude sermon; it's a grace sermon. It's about the graciousness of God—His grace toward you and me.

In verse 48, Jesus says, *Be ye therefore perfect, even as your Father which is in heaven is perfect.*

If Jesus said, *Be ye therefore perfect,* that means we need to be perfect! It isn't just a good idea or a beautiful thought; it's a commandment. Our minds have a hard time grasping that concept, because such a truth must be spiritually discerned.

If someone asked, "Are you as perfect as God?", what would your reaction be? The very suggestion that we poor, frail humans might be perfect as Almighty God seems almost sacrilegious. Yet, Jesus not only said we *can* be; He commanded us to be!

Let's see if our Bible definition of the word *perfect* will hold true for God. Remember our definition of *perfect:* the removal of all that is wanting.

Has all the wrong been removed from God? There was never any wrong in Him to remove!

Have all God's needs been supplied? He is *El Shaddai*, the Supreme Supplier of all things.

Obviously, the word *perfect* holds true for God.

The word *perfect* also means mature. Is there any question in your mind about God's being mature? Or complete? Or without spot or blemish? No doubt about it: God is perfect.

Yet Jesus tells us—you and me—to be perfect as God is perfect. He is saying we can have all of our needs met and any wrong removed from our hearts. How can that be?

The Ministry of Perfection

We have read from 2 Timothy 3:16,17:

All scripture is given by inspiration of God, and is profitable for doctrine, for reproof, for correction, for instruction in righteousness: That the man of God may be perfect.

The Word of God is given to perfect the saints. But as the Apostle Paul points out, the work of ''saint perfecting'' is reserved for the fivefold ministry:

As he gave some, apostles; and some, prophets; and some, evangelists; and some, pastors and teachers; for the perfecting of the saints (Eph. 4:11,12).

The ministry uses the Word of God to accomplish its work of perfecting the saints. If, in the entire life-span of my ministry, I can help but one person to somehow ''be perfect,'' I will feel that I have fulfilled my calling.

That is the kind of attitude Jesus had. The only difference is, He did it!

In His Image

Jesus said to us, *Be ye therefore perfect, even as your Father in heaven is perfect.* We know that God is higher than us. He is the Everlasting Father, the Creator of heaven and earth.

But you and I are made in His likeness, in His image. We are partakers of His life here on earth. We can be perfect like He is; only our perfection will be on a somewhat smaller scale.

Let me give you an example. I have a friend in the ministry, a singer named David. He has a little boy named Joshua. Dave and his son look alike. As an image of David, little Joshua is perfect. But he isn't as strong as his father. He can't drive a car like his dad. He can't sing like his dad. Yet he is still the perfect image of Dave.

You and I are the perfect image of our heavenly Father. We may not be able to do what He can, but as far as God is concerned, we're His perfect image.

As God is in heaven, so are we on earth. (1 John 4:17.) God's will is to be done *in earth, as it is in heaven* (Matt. 6:10). In this world, we are Jesus. We are the ''express image'' of our heavenly Father. We are God in the earth. According to Genesis 1:26, we were created by God in His image and likeness. The Hebrew word for *likeness* literally means an image, such as in a mirror.

In the spiritual sense, we are perfect. We have been *made* perfect, and we can *be* perfect, even as our Father is perfect. The very life force within us proceeds from God. It is His life with the perfection that He is.

Love is the perfection of God, and His compassion and mercy are the glory of His being. Because of the compassion and mercy of God, you became His love-child. Therefore, as He is perfect, so are you. John caught hold of this concept when he wrote in his epistle: *As he is, so are we in this world* (1 John 4:17).

If someone were to say to you, "Show me God and I'll believe," you should be able to simply say, like Jesus, "If you've seen me, you've seen the Father."

If you think, *Oh, I couldn't say that!* then your heart isn't perfect yet. But it can be. And it will be if you allow this truth from God's Word to sink down into your spirit.

It is possible for a believer to walk into a hospital room and say to the sick, "I have good news! Jesus Christ of Nazareth is here. It's time to lay hands on you, so you can rise up and walk."

We can have that boldness only when we get our hearts perfected as God is perfect—fully relying on Him and trusting in Him, fully persuaded that He is working in us because of a perfect heart. That perfection comes not because of anything we do, but because of what we are in Christ Jesus.

God has told me, "I want My people to be perfect, to have perfect hearts." He is looking for perfect hearts through whom and to whom He can show Himself strong.

You **can** have a perfect heart, absolutely cleansed of all wrong, all needs supplied. You can be perfect, even as your Father in heaven is perfect. Jesus said so!

5

A Heart Like God's

Now we will see some of the attributes of a heart like God's. Then we will be better able to understand how we can develop ours to be like His.

1. Love

God's heart is a heart of love. A person whose heart is as perfect as God's will be a lover. When you love someone, you can forgive him, even when he makes mistakes and hurts you. That is how God's heart is toward us. Jesus said:

But I say unto you which hear, Love your enemies, do good to them which hate you,

Bless them that curse you, and pray for them which despitefully use you.
                    Luke 6:27,28

"Love your enemies." Is this an unreasonable demand? God isn't requiring of us anything that He Himself hasn't already done many times. He has loved His enemies far more than we could even imagine. People have cursed Him, rejected Him, rebelled against Him, and blamed Him for all kinds of evil. Yet He has always maintained a heart of love toward them.

The scripture that says it best is John 3:16. *God so loved the world, that he gave his only begotten Son.* His Son prayed for His enemies at the very moment they were crucifying Him. *Father forgive them; for they know not what they do* (Luke 23:34).

A true heart, perfected as God's, is full of love, even for its enemies. Love is being ready to give your life for your enemies. That's what Jesus did. He came to earth for only one reason: to give His life.

Bless them that curse you, and pray for them that despitefully use you.

And unto him that smiteth thee on the one cheek offer also the other, and him that taketh away thy cloke forbid not to take thy coat also.

Give to every man that asketh of thee; and of him that taketh away thy goods ask them not again.

And as ye would that men should do to you, do ye also to them likewise.

For if ye love them which love you, what thank have ye? for sinners also love those that love them.

And if ye do good to them which do good to you, what thank have ye? for sinners also do even the same.

And if ye lend to them of whom ye hope to receive, what thank have ye? for sinners also lend to sinners, to receive as much again.

But love ye your enemies, and do good, and lend, hoping for nothing again; and your reward shall be great, and ye shall be the children of the Highest: for he is kind unto the unthankful and to the evil.

Luke 6:28-35

The reward Jesus is talking about here is that you will have a heart of love. You will be a love-child.

Colossians 3:14 calls love "the bond of perfectness." The bond of *all* perfection is love. God's love is His perfection, and His love is your perfection when it's residing within you.

So the first attribute, or mark, of a heart as perfect as God's is love.

2. Mercy and Compassion

In Luke 6:36, Jesus says, *Be ye therefore merciful, as your Father also is merciful.* God is full of compassion and tender mercy.

When you and I would want to give up on people and totally destroy them, God deals with them mercifully.

Most "good" Christians look at sinners and say, "He's been so mean and rotten. I hope all hell falls on him, so he'll come to God!" But do you know what really draws sinners to repentance? Not tragedy or destruction. Romans 2:4 says that the goodness of God draws all men to repentance. You should deal mercifully with such people and love them. Remember, mercy and compassion are the glory of God's being, and that mercy and compassion should be residing within you.

If we didn't have the life and Spirit of Jesus within us, we could say that God's mercy and compassion are beyond our realm. But God took care of that. He sent Jesus as a human example to prove that we can be merciful and compassionate, just as He was. Jesus was a man, who was tempted in all ways as we are. (Heb. 4:15.) But He was faithful, a faithful and compassionate High Priest. He proved that mercy and compassion are possible in the human realm.

3. Humility

When your heart becomes perfected as God's, you don't get proud, you get humble.

Just as love is God's perfection, humility was Jesus' perfection. Jesus said, *The Son of man came not to be ministered unto, but to minister* (Matt. 20:28). Jesus came to earth to minister, to give His life for others.

The mark of humility is a willingness to serve. A truly humble heart empties itself and relies totally on God. Jesus came as a servant. He didn't exercise lordship in a dominating spirit; He exercised servantship in a loving spirit of humility by ministering to people.

Humility doesn't make you into a weakling. It makes you bold. Humility carries power. Jesus wasn't fragile; He was full of dynamic power. Yet, He was humility in operation.

4. Obedience

In Chapter 3 we saw that obedience was made up of three parts: to hear, to comprehend, and to execute. We hear in the mental or soulish realm. We understand or comprehend in the spiritual realm. We put action to the command in the physical realm.

Now I want to emphasize the opposite of obey: to disobey.

In both the Old and New Testaments, to disobey actually means to bitterly oppose or openly rebel.

Someone may say, ''Wait a minute. I don't oppose God. I'm not rebelling against Him." If you're disobedient to His Word, you are.

When our children don't obey us, we say they are rebellious. Yet, when it comes to our disobedience to God, we wouldn't dare label it rebellion. But it's the same thing. When God says do something, we must do it. If not, we are opposing and openly rebelling against Him.

Let me give you an example of disobedience from the Scriptures. In 1 Samuel, chapter 15, we find the story of Saul and Samuel. Samuel anointed Saul as king over Israel and told him, "God says for you to destroy the Amalekites. Drive them out of the land. Kill them all. Don't spare any." (1 Sam. 15:1-4.)

That may seem rather harsh or cruel by today's standards, but God had a reason. These people represented a type of sin to Him. He ordered them totally destroyed so that sin could be wiped out forever.

Saul conquered the Amalekites and killed all of them except the king. Also he had been commanded to kill all of the animals, but he spared the best of the sheep and oxen.

Samuel, the prophet, came to him and said, "You have disobeyed God." True to form, Saul did what every disobedient person does—he passed the buck!

And Saul said unto Samuel, Yea, I have obeyed the voice of the Lord, and have gone the way which the Lord sent me, and have brought Agag the king of Amalek, and have utterly destroyed the Amalekites.

But the people took of the spoil, sheep and oxen.

1 Samuel 15:20,21

"Oh, I was obedient to the Lord, Samuel. It was the people who did this thing!"

The first sign of a disobedient heart is an attempt to lay the blame for our actions on someone else. "*He* did it!" or "*She* did it!" Saul was in disobedience, and he knew it, so he tried to lay the blame on someone else.

What was Samuel's response to all this? We read it in verse 23: *For rebellion is as the sin of witchcraft, and stubbornness is as iniquity and idolatry.*

In God's sight, to be disobedient is the same as bowing down before a pagan idol.

5. A Giving Heart

In the 19th chapter of Matthew, we read about a rich young man who came to Jesus and asked, *Good Master, what good thing shall I do, that I may have eternal life?* (Matt. 19:16).

Jesus answered by asking him, *Why callest thou me good? there is none good but*

one, that is, God: but if thou wilt enter into
life, keep the commandments* (v. 17).

To this, the rich young ruler replied,
*All these things have I kept from my youth
up: what lack I yet?* (v. 20). This is why he
was rich: He had kept God's
commandments. If you will keep God's
commandments and statutes, the
blessings of God will overtake you.
(Deut. 28:1,2.)

Now let's look at what Jesus said to
him in the 21st verse: *Jesus said unto him,
If thou wilt be **perfect**, go and sell that thou
hast, and give to the poor, and thou shalt
have treasure in heaven: and come and
follow me.*

He was saying, "If you want to be
perfect—totally without wrong, with
every need supplied—sell what you
have and give to the poor."

You can't outgive God. Jesus didn't
want this young man to do without. He
wasn't trying to deprive him of his

goods or possessions. He just wanted him to have a perfect heart. Jesus had the spirit of a servant, a giving spirit. Here He tells the rich young ruler, ''If you want to be perfect, you'll be a giver like God is.''

Show me a stingy Christian, and I'll show you a person without a perfect heart. In 1 Corinthians 5:11, Paul tells us to stay away from stingy (or covetous) people and not to fellowship with them. The reason is that such people will begin to affect us. We become like those with whom we fellowship. (1 Cor. 5:6.) We need to fellowship with people who are givers and be givers ourselves, because God is a giver.

6. A Spiritual Attitude

For spiritual fruit to be produced in our lives, we must be spiritual.

But the natural man receiveth not the things of the Spirit of God: for they are foolishness unto him: neither can he know them, because they are spiritually discerned.

But he that is spiritual judgeth all things, yet he himself is judged of no man.

For who hath known the mind of the Lord, that he may instruct him? But we have the mind of Christ.

And I, brethren, could not speak unto you as unto spiritual, but as unto carnal, even as unto babes in Christ.

1 Corinthians 2:14-16; 3:1

You may ask, ''What's the difference between a spiritual person and a carnal person?''

Paul said that those who are carnal have to be fed with milk. (1 Cor. 3:2.) The word *judgeth* in verse 15 above means to discern. A carnal person is one who does not discern spiritual things. The Corinthians were born-again, Spirit-filled Christians who operated in the gifts of the Spirit; but they weren't perfect. They were still carnal.

A spiritual person is one who discerns the Word of God. He rightly divides the Word and puts it into action in his life. A spiritual person has the mind of Christ.

First Corinthians 1:10 says: *Now I beseech you, brethren, by the name of our Lord Jesus Christ, that ye all speak the same thing, and that there be no divisions among you; but that ye be perfectly joined together in the same mind and in the same judgment.*

A spiritual person is one who doesn't have envy, strife, or contention in his life. When we get our hearts perfected before God, we really become true spiritual beings. Real spirituality is not outward; it's inward. God looks not upon our actions, but upon our hearts.

7. A Desire for the Perfection of Others

Paul ended his letters to the Corinthian church with this prayer for them:

Now I pray to God that ye do no evil . . . For we can do nothing against the truth, but for the truth.

For we are glad, when we are weak, and ye are strong: and this also we wish (or pray), *even your perfection.*

2 Corinthians 13:7-9

The true mark of a heart like God's is a willingness to pray for other people to be perfected. You won't always be praying for yourself: "Oh, God, perfect *me*. Make *me* perfect." Your true prayer will be for others: "Father, perfect *them*." A perfect heart is one which considers others first.

Therefore I write these things being absent, lest being present I should use sharpness, according to the power which the Lord hath given me to edification, and not to destruction.

Finally, brethren, farewell. Be perfect, be of good comfort, be of one mind, live in peace; and the God of love and peace shall be with you.

> *2 Corinthians 13:10,11*

Most of us will say, "Thank God, we can be comforted. We can have peace and be of one mind." But no one will dare to say, "Thank God, we can be perfect."

Yet, Paul wrote to the people at Corinth, *Finally, brethren, farewell. **Be perfect.*** His aim was to see them brought to perfection. That should be our aim as well.

The main goal of any person called into the fivefold ministry of Jesus Christ should be to see perfection in the Body of Christ. Every minister—apostles, prophets, evangelists, pastors, and teachers—should be praying that the people be perfected.

Remember, perfection means having all that's wrong removed and all that's wanted supplied. To be perfected is to have a supply of divine health furnished to the physical body. To be perfected is to live in God's abundant prosperity, having every need supplied. To be perfected is to be saved, filled with God's Spirit, and living a life of peace, contentment, and power in the Holy Ghost.

Jesus said, ''Be perfect,'' so let's do it! Paul prayed for people to be perfected, so let's do it! Once we are walking in that realm of perfection, our desire will be to see the perfection of others.

8. Strive To Be Like Jesus

. . . If by any means I might attain unto the resurrection of the dead.

Not as though I had already attained, either were already perfect: but I follow after, if that I may apprehend that for which also I am apprehended of Christ Jesus.

Brethren, I count not myself to have apprehended: but this one thing I do, forgetting those things which are behind, and reaching forth unto those things which are before,

I press toward the mark for the prize of the high calling of God in Christ Jesus.

Let us therefore, as many as be perfect, be thus minded: and if in any thing ye be otherwise minded, God shall reveal even this unto you.

Nevertheless, whereto we have already attained, let us walk by the same rule, let us mind the same thing.

Brethren, be followers together of me, and mark them which walk so as ye have us for an ensample.

Philippians 3:11-17

Paul said, "Even though I may not have obtained all yet, I have obtained some things. And those of you who would be perfect, be of the same mind.'' Paul had set as his goal the high calling of God in Christ Jesus.

Our goal should be perfection in Christ Jesus—to be more like Jesus tomorrow than we are today. To do that, we must refuse to look at the mistakes we made in the past. We must keep our eyes set on the goal ahead of us: to walk perfect before God, even though our actions may not always be perfect.

Have you ever seen a marathon runner who is satisfied with the race he has run? As good as it may have been, he is never satisfied. He always wants to beat his own record. He says, ''I can beat that. Next time I'll do better.''

A person with a perfected heart realizes he is in a race. He knows he will finish his course, but he also knows he can perfect it even more.

That's the way you and I should be in our Christian walk. The better our race seems to be, the more we should strive for perfection.

Be ye perfect, **even as** *your Father in heaven is perfect*. Is God perfect? Is He walking in health? Is He prosperous and successful? Is His life in heaven abundant and full and glorious? Does He live in perfection? The answer is an emphatic **yes!**

God's will is done perfectly in heaven, and Jesus prayed that His will be done *in earth, as it is in heaven*. That means it is God's will that this earth be perfect for us. We can walk in the same fullness, abundance, power, and peace on earth as God does in heaven.

It is the desire of my heart, my prayer above all else, that every person who reads these words might be perfected in every area of their lives—spirit, soul, and body. I pray that everything wrong in your heart and life might be removed, that every need be supplied through our Lord and Savior

Jesus Christ. To Him be honor and glory forever and ever!

6
Perfect In Christ Jesus

To whom God would make known what is the riches of his glory of this mystery among the Gentiles; which is Christ in you, the hope of glory:

Whom we preach, warning every man, and teaching every man in all wisdom; that we may present every man perfect in Christ Jesus.

Colossians 1:27,28

When the mystery of Christ in us, the hope of glory, is ministered to people, it causes them to be presented perfect in Christ Jesus.

By the which will we are sanctified through the offering of the body of Jesus Christ once for all.

And every priest standeth daily ministering and offering oftentimes the same sacrifices, which can never take away sins:

But this man (Christ Jesus), *after he had offered one sacrifice for sins for ever, sat down on the right hand of God;*

From henceforth expecting till his enemies be made his footstool.

For by one offering he hath perfected for ever them that are sanctified.

Hebrews 10:10-14

Jesus is expecting you and me to tap into His sanctification, causing perfection to flow in our lives. He is expecting us to take hold of sanctification through the offering of His blood and preach perfection to the world.

Hebrews is not just a book contrasting the Old and New Covenants. The message of Hebrews is that no one can be made perfect, or perfected, by the Old Testament sacrifices. Hebrews 7:19 says, *For the law made nothing perfect.* In Hebrews 10:4 we are told, *For it is not possible that the blood of bulls and of goats should take away sins.* But rather, as we see in verse 14, *For by one offering he* (Jesus) *hath perfected for ever them that are sanctified.*

The words *perfect* and *perfected* are used more times in Hebrews than in the entire Bible. Hebrews is telling us that what the Old Testament law and sacrifices could not do, Jesus has done for us through His sacrifice and the shedding of His blood on the cross at Calvary.

By His perfect sacrifices, Jesus has forevermore offered you and me as perfect before God. We have been made perfect in Christ Jesus.

Now the God of peace, that brought again from the dead our Lord Jesus, that great shepherd of the sheep, through the blood of the everlasting covenant,

Make you perfect in every good work to do his will, working in you that which is wellpleasing in his sight, through Jesus Christ; to whom be glory for ever and ever. Amen.

Hebrews 13:20,21

Would you agree that Jesus has already died and been raised from the dead? No question about it! Therefore, by the blood of an everlasting covenant that has already been established, He has made us perfect. It's already been done.

The writer of Hebrews has summed up everything by saying that Jesus Christ of Nazareth—the complete fullness of the Godhead, the perfect sacrifice—has made us perfect **in** Him. As members of the Body of Christ, we have been made perfect. That is an accomplished fact. We're not working to be perfect; we already are perfect **in Him.**

As He Is . . .

We can see by the authority of the Word of God that all things necessary for our sanctification (or perfection) have already been fulfilled in Christ Jesus.

Colossians 2:9,10 tells us, *For in him dwelleth all the fulness of the Godhead bodily. And ye are complete in Him.*

Because *as he is, so are we in this world* (1 John 4:17).

Jesus is complete, so are we complete. He is perfect, so are we perfect. We are completed, and perfected in Christ Jesus.

When Jesus walked the earth, we were in Him. When He walked in obedience, ministering to the sick, being made perfect through suffering, God saw us in Him fulfilled and complete. (Heb. 5:7-9.)

When Jesus died, we died with Him. When He was ushered into the lowest pits of pain and agony, we were in Him. (Ps. 7; 22; 89.)

But good news! After three days and nights, He arose victorious over sin, death, hell, and the grave. And we arose with Him—victorious! Jesus' victory was *our* victory!

God didn't speak the words of resurrection to Jesus alone; He spoke them to you and me. That's the mystery of Christ in us, the hope of glory, spoken of in Colossians 1:27. The mystery in our minds is how we could have died with Him and been crucified with Him. (See Rom. 6:6; Gal. 2:20.) But it's true because God said it.

When Jesus was quickened and made alive, we were made alive in Him, raised up together in Him. (Eph. 1:20; 2:6.) When He broke hell wide open and stripped Satan of his authority, making a show of him openly, you and I were right there with Him. (Col. 2:13-15.) We were just as much in Him then as we are now. Glory to God!

According to Ephesians 2:5,6, we have been made to sit together with Him in heavenly places. We are seated *far above all principality, and power, and might, and dominion, and every name that is named . . . in this world* (Eph. 1:20,21).

We are sitting far above all these things because we've been made perfect in Christ Jesus. When Jesus was resurrected, we were resurrected. When He was re-created, we were re-created. When He was made perfect, we were made perfect. Perfection is an accomplished fact.

Paul wrote in Ephesians 1:3, *Blessed be the God and Father of our Lord Jesus Christ, who hath blessed us with all spiritual blessings in heavenly places in Christ.* God has delivered us out of the kingdom of darkness and has translated us into the Kingdom of His dear Son.

(Col. 1:13.) We have stepped from darkness into light. When Jesus, the Light of the world, dispelled darkness in our behalf, we became light.

All things are already ours. Romans 8:32 says that God freely gives us all things. Paul wrote in 1 Corinthians 3:21, *All things are yours.* Christ is the Head; we are the Body. All things have been given to Him by God, so everything He has is ours. We already have everything we need in Christ Jesus—salvation; prosperity; healing; soundness of spirit, mind, and body.

Our Fight of Faith

The fight of faith is not a fight to obtain; it is a fight to keep. We are fighting to keep Satan from stealing what is already ours. Faith thus becomes not so much an offensive weapon, as a defensive shield.

Satan wants to steal away our confidence in being perfect, so he tries to embed doubt in our spirits. We must use our faith to keep our image of perfection and allow it to manifest.

In principle, we have already been made perfect. In practice, we have yet to be perfected. In principle, according to Hebrews 10:14, those who are sanctified have been made perfect by the sacrifice of Jesus.

First Corinthians 1:30 says, *But of him are ye in Christ Jesus, who of God is made unto us wisdom, and righteousness, and sanctification, and redemption.* If Jesus is the Lord of your life, you are in Him. You have been made righteous. You have been redeemed. You have been made wisdom. You have been sanctified.

Our fight of faith lies in holding on to all that has already been provided by the blood sacrifice of Jesus.

7

Perfection As A Seed

Perfection is imparted to us by the Holy Spirit. When you made Jesus the Lord of your life, a new birth took place in your spirit by an inner action of the Word of God and the Spirit of God.

In John 3:2, Nicodemus, a ruler of the Jews, came to Jesus and said, "Lord, we know that You are a teacher sent from God, because of the miracles You do."

Jesus answered, "I tell you, in order to enter the Kingdom of God, you must be born again."

Then Nicodemus asked, "How can I enter into my mother's womb again?"

Jesus replied, *Except a man be born of water and of the Spirit, he cannot enter into the kingdom of God* (v. 5).

The water He was speaking about is the Word of God. You are born again by the Word and by the Spirit. According to Ephesians 5:26,27, you have been cleansed, sanctified, and presented unto God by the washing of the water of the Word.

In John 15:3, Jesus told His disciples, *Now ye are clean through the word which I have spoken unto you.* The water of the Word washes and cleanses you; then you are born of the Spirit to become a new creation. Titus 3:5 says that we are saved *by the washing of regeneration, and renewing of the Holy Ghost.*

When you were born again, it was by a seed. The Word was the seed that brought forth life in your spirit.

A tree does not just materialize in your front yard. To produce a tree, you must plant a seed. That seed has life within it; and if planted in the right soil, it will bring forth a tree.

Perfection is a seed. When you were born again, the Holy Spirit imparted to you an incorruptible seed—the Word of God—which has within it the ability to grow and bring forth perfection.

Any farmer knows the basic laws of nature. If a seed is planted in the ground, it doesn't spring into a full-grown plant overnight, like Jack's beanstalk. A seed grows gradually. First it appears as a blade, then as a stalk, then it becomes a full ear of corn. (Mark 4:26-28.)

Perfection in the Lord Jesus Christ—having all that's wrong removed and all that's wanted supplied—has been planted as a seed. It takes time for that seed of perfection to grow and develop, producing fruit.

Within most people, whether born again or not, is a desire to do right, even though their flesh may be telling them to do wrong. According to Hebrews 10:16, God writes His laws in our hearts and in our minds. It has already been done. It is a law, a seed, that is operating and working within us. But that seed must be nurtured and cared for; otherwise, the cares of this world, the deceitfulness of riches, and the lusts of other things will choke it and keep it from bringing forth fruit to perfection. (Mark 4:19.)

A seed of perfection was planted in your spirit when you were born again. That seed is pushing its way up, wanting to spring forth as a blade, then a stalk, then into a full fruit of perfection. The Kingdom of God operates that way, just as a seed matures and grows.

When people brought some little children to Jesus for Him to bless, the disciples tried to stop them, but He said, *Suffer the little children to come unto me* (Mark 10:14). When the children were brought to Him, He blessed them and said, *Whosoever shall not receive the kingdom of God as a little child, he shall not enter therein* (v. 15).

To receive the Kingdom of God as a little child means to receive it as a seed that is planted within us. A child is first conceived as a seed in the womb. Then it matures and develops, finally issuing forth as a baby. The baby grows and develops. He buds and brings forth fruit, becoming a child. Then the child continues to grow to adulthood.

To receive the Kingdom as a little child means to receive it as a seed, then to let that seed grow like a child within us. No one expects a tiny baby to be like an adult. It takes time for the maturing process to be completed.

The Kingdom of God works the same way. It is as a child. It grows, matures, and produces fruit based on the care and nurture it receives.

Receive the Kingdom of God as a seed and allow it to grow within you.

Perfect Patience At Work

Perfect patience makes a perfect heart.

In the eighth chapter of Luke, Jesus is describing the types of soil into which the Word falls. In verse 15, He says: *But that on the good ground are they, which in an honest and good heart, having heard the word, keep it, and bring forth fruit* **with patience.**

The Greek translation says, ''Bring forth fruit to perfection with patience.'' Often we start bringing forth fruit, then get impatient because more fruit doesn't come. We stop sowing and start devouring the fruit that has ripened, thereby destroying the very seed we must have to produce more fruit.

Sowing and reaping is a spiritual law that works. But it requires patience to reap what we have sown.

What is patience? A mother of eight rowdy kids once told me that patience was not killing one of them! But that isn't patience. That's just teeth-clinching endurance. Real patience is enduring long with the confidence of faith producing.

Let's see what James had to say about patience.

My brethren, count it all joy when ye fall into divers temptations;

Knowing this, that the trying of your faith worketh patience.

James 1:2,3

Reading this passage in only the *King James Version* prevents us from fully understanding the concept of patience that is embodied in the original Greek text. The Greek says, ''Brethren, there are temptations encircling you at all times.''

You will have opportunities for temptations, tests, and trials every day of your life, everywhere you go. But if you put your faith to work with patience, those trials and temptations will have no effect! Let's read on:

But let patience have her perfect work, that ye may be perfect and entire, wanting nothing.

James 1:4

Remember the definition of *perfect:* the removal of all that's wrong, the supplying of all that's wanted. Although temptations, tests, and trials are all around us, we can count it all joy because patience is bringing forth fruit to perfection in our lives. Then we will be perfect and entire, wanting nothing!

If we will put patience to work for us, we can walk in the fullness of joy even in the midst of temptations, tests, and trials. We know that our joy has been made full when we abide in Him. Patience is working, and the seed of perfection is growing within us.

Patience is the force which brings about that perfection.

8

The Perfect Tongue

For in many things we offend all. If any man offend not in word, the same is a perfect man, and able also to bridle the whole body.
James 3:2

One true mark of a perfected heart is a perfect tongue, the ability to offend no one in word. Jesus was perfect. Every word that came from His mouth was perfect. By speaking what He says, our tongues will be perfect, too.

"If any person can bridle his tongue, he can bridle his whole body," says James. That is the mark of maturity.

When no corrupt communication proceeds from your mouth except that which edifies and ministers grace to the hearer, then you can know that you have achieved perfection. When you can control your tongue, you will be a perfect man.

Perfection seems so far away, yet it's so close. That little member in your mouth has residing within it your perfection. You have been made perfect, but you need to be perfected. The thing that does it is your words.

Your words are a consuming fire. They can bring life, health, victory, deliverance, and edification; or they can bring death, sickness, defeat, bondage, and destruction.

The Tongue of Fire

Even so the tongue is a little member and boasteth great things. Behold, how great a matter a little fire kindleth!

And the tongue is a fire, a world of iniquity: so is the tongue among our

*members, that it defileth the whole body,
and setteth on fire the course of nature; and
it is set on fire of hell.*

James 3:5,6

Note the phrase, "set on fire of
hell." A tongue set on fire of hell is a
world of iniquity. The tongue sets on
fire the course of nature in our lives.

Well, I have good news for you: If
the tongue is an agency of hell-fire, it
can also be set on fire of heaven!

In Jeremiah 5:14 God said, *Because ye
speak this word, behold, I will make my
words in thy mouth fire.* In Jeremiah
23:29, He asks, *Is not my word like as a
fire?* In Isaiah, chapters 6 and 30, God
talks about His Word in our mouths as a
fire.

A tongue that is bridled and perfect
becomes a tongue set on fire of heaven.
Instead of a world of iniquity, it
becomes a world of righteousness.

When our tongues are speaking God's Word, they become a fire that not only perfects our bodies, but creates an entire world of righteousness in our midst.

James 3:6 says that the tongue *defileth* the whole body.

Just as a person with an unbridled tongue *defiles* his body, a person with a bridled tongue *perfects* and *cleanses* his body.

The Tongue of Perfection

Your words determine the level of perfection that you attain in your life.

As you speak according to the Word of God, your words will bring forth fruit unto perfection. Everything wrong will be removed and everything needed will be supplied. The perfect tongue will produce the perfect life.

As we take hold of this truth, the entire Body of Christ will come together, perfected. When that day of perfection comes, then our Lord will come to take us home with Him. (1 Thess. 4:16,17.) We will know the fullness of perfection. We will see Him as He is and be changed into the perfect image of Christ. What a day that will be!

Conclusion

When the seed of God's Word is planted, it grows. Through this book, seeds have been planted in you. Nurture them. Water them. God will give the increase. As that increase comes, it will bring forth fruit. Small though it may be at first, keep bringing it forth. It will get bigger and bigger. Eventually it will become such a part of you that you will become a seed planter—a perfectionist.

There's nothing wrong with being a perfectionist. Practice makes perfect. The same holds true in the Word of God. Practice the Word, and it will make you perfect. Practice speaking the Word; it will perfect you.

A perfect tongue produces perfect faith. Perfect faith applied with perfect patience makes a perfect heart, leads you on a perfect way, and produces a perfect man.

You are made perfect in Jesus Christ. Now act perfect!

Billy Rash made Jesus the Lord of his life in September 1974 and received the infilling of the Holy Spirit in January 1976. After being introduced to the faith message through the ministry of Kenneth Copeland, Billy, his wife Joan, and their two sons began growing in the knowledge of God's Word.

Between 1975 and 1978 Joan underwent brain surgery three times. During this time, Billy and his family realized the importance of placing their trust and confidence in God to meet their needs in every area. Because they applied

Scriptures on divine health to Joan's condition, she was healed!

Left thousands of dollars in debt from hospital expenses, they again placed their confidence in God and His Word. By putting God's laws of prosperity to work, they were completely out of debt within a year.

Billy worked with Kenneth Copeland Ministries for four years. For three of those years, he served as Associate Minister and assisted Brother Copeland, ministering with him in seminars across the country. Today Billy ministers on his own, taking the uncompromising Word of God to the world.

You may contact Billy Rash by writing:

Billy Rash
P. O. Box 79506
Fort Worth, TX 76179

For additional copies of *The Perfected Heart*, write:

HARRISON HOUSE
P. O. Box 35035 • Tulsa, OK 74153